My Blooming Stars

Charlie Belle

Grosvenor House
Publishing Limited

This book is published by
Grosvenor House Publishing Ltd
Link House
140 The Broadway, Tolworth, Surrey, KT6 7HT.
www.grosvenorhousepublishing.co.uk

A CIP record for this book
is available from the British Library

ISBN 978-1-80381-916-7

"To little me: you were never listened to.
This is how I made you heard"

Chapter 1

Marigold – suffering

I am not my mother's child.
Nor am I my father's.
They'll only ever be rotten apples.
And yet,
It's as though I was picked from an entirely different tree.
I am not my mother's child and that is something I'll wear proud.
If that makes a baby of the earth or the sun then so be it.
But I am no child of theirs.

– a strangers baby

Although he's so far away, I still feel his eyes watching.
It's always from the places you'd expect, too.
The crack of my wardrobe open just a bit,
or the shadows created by my hanging clothes.
I sometimes think I see him too.
In the darkness behind my door,
or the blur in the corner of eyes.
It seems that even if i'm not scared of ghosts or zombies
anymore,
I'll always be scared of him.

– childhood monsters

I did everything I could.
I screamed.
I shouted.
I fought for us all.
But no one heard me.
Well, no.
No one listened.
I don't know what hurts more;
the fact I was ignored or
that I didn't get an apology.

– too young to know

I can still hear her screams.
She begs for you to stop.
The glasses thrown,
the music turned up to drown out their echoes.
No one knew, but me.
I made everything better;
I was the peace keeper.
I held a mothers hands,
as she cradled me in her bleeding arms.
I watched his tears fall as he apologised over and over.
She kissed my forehead,
losing myself in sleep.
And just like the family inside the smashed photo frame,
we pretended everything was okay.

She was an unfortunate miracle,
a blessing that will haunt me every day of my life.
She taught me what not to be,
she showed me all the secrets I was supposed to be kept from.
I'd hold her while she mingled with the demons she fought,
and watched when they'd inevitably burn her.

The adult in me thanks her,
for guiding me to my true family.
She taught me how to not raise my future children.

But the child I am cries because of her.
I've no childhood worth of salvation,
and too much hurt to heal.

Children I did not grow,
or bring into this world,
were mine to raise.
They'd cry to me,
in the absence of you.
I'd catch their tears,
and kiss them goodnight.
I covered their eyes from the mess you made of yourself,
and sung them to sleep.
I kept them safe on the days you would not.
I have loved them like a mother and father,
since the day you stopped.

You were spearmint toothpaste,
the smell of summer.
You were the treehouses,
the story telling.
You were the undying imagination,
the tomfoolery.
You were the sickness that sweetened the sours of him.
You were the blind eye for my mind when he played tricks.
For when he danced with the devil all the night until dawn struck his eyes.
You were the melodies my heart sang,
to drown out his haunting cries.

– childhood

To exist as too little and too much
is far too cruel.
Too much stomach and not enough hip,
not enough chest but too much leg.
To have the perfect balance to satisfy the needs of those
who have no value of me is my hardest challenge in life.
But when it is too much weight lost and not enough in
my tummy,
I am still not enough.

It is as though the devil wishes to humour me.
When I cannot find it within myself to eat,
the darkness will eat me.
Every thought.
Every lesser number.
Every god damn hour that passes and still not a crumb
of food;
it consumes me.
The overwhelming guilt that fills me up,
that which makes me cry all the nights
and tires me all the days.

Do they notice it too?
How it spills over my skirt and tightens my top.
How it rips itself apart to fit the ever growing
monstrosity that is my body.
How, the artwork I drew begin to fade from my arms.
My most favourite paintings don't stay forever.
It leaves, and forgets.
Even after all those days and nights,
it's as though my hurt never existed at all.

– skin

You'll never know the feeling of looking in the mirror
and not fitting the frame.
Or having to go to the back of the shelf
because you're not small enough to be put at the front.
You'll never know what it's like believing that there is
too much of you to love.
Or being constantly reminded by society that even
though you're 4 sizes too big,
you're still not enough.

– smaller girls

"love has no shape"

What a lie that was.
Love is small,
so incredibly small.
Love is a UK size 6.
Love has long hair and bright eyes,
a thigh gap and slim arms.
Love has round hips and a flat tummy,
a hairless physique and plump lips.

Love is impossible.

It was a smile that broke her heart.
Because she knew it was only a smile.
No hidden romance along his cupid's bow.
No kiss in the corner of his lips.
It was just a smile,
and that all it will ever be.

– unrequited

I can only apologise to you.
For the fullest of promises,
now emptying out.
For the supposed truths I told you.
For the times I said I'd get you home,
but never did.

I will crave that home the way you do,
the idea of them often seemed too good.
Yet you deserve that love,
but do I?

The me that you have become.
Is she worthy of that?
After the mistakes,
the self hatred,
the fear that started a fire too strong to survive.
Is she someone deserving of that home?

I am so sorry.

You're my therapy.
The coping I need.
When the simplicity of endless hunger,
or of bleeding
or crying
is far too complicated,
I write.

Chapter 2

Cyclamen – heartache

To be loved by a writer is the greatest blessing you'll get.
If you hold their heart for long enough,
they'll create such a string of words to perfectly envelope the feeling of your embrace.
But if you dare to shatter it,
the only form of motivation to write will be sourced from hurt.
From anger and sadness.
And that will be your biggest regret.
Her chorus will haunt your
ears until they deafen you.
Those lyrics will scar your soul for its entire existence.

I'll live everyday to figure out how to get you into these pages.
How I can create a string of words so beautiful that they resemble you.
That they make someone feel so strongly as I do for you.

You'll always be the poetry I wish I could write.

The remanence you have left on heart is one
I will never rid myself of.
Your impact on me has shaped my very being.
For better or for worse?
I don't quite know.
But, your love was unique.
My soul is littered with pretty little reminders of you.
Unfillable craters in my heart.
They ache with your absence.
It's not a pain that stings, or hurts.
It's just a numbness I wish I could dispose of.
But if that were so, I'd lose myself of you.

– I could never do that.

I think that more often than not,
she would be disappointed in me.
The fact that despite the odds she got us out.
She did all she could to help her children.
But the people they turned into
are people who are hurt.
Babies broken by the parents who couldn't do it.
They live their days in a sense of loss,
an endless loop of questions unknown.
The gods themselves lack the answers we all seek so badly.
My only job was to protect them,
to shield them from the things they couldn't control.

I didn't do enough;
I should've done more.

I cannot bring myself to blame anyone else but myself
for the fact that my children are hurting.
The babies I did not grow,
were the ones I nurtured
in the empty home we were in.

I often wished I could somehow prove how much my inner child hurt,
that somehow I could physicalise her.
But when I look at the body I live in,
I see her presence.
I see the drawing she makes,
the ones that shine in the sun.
The carvings she'd leave on my curves,
to make herself known.
Her sketches trail all over,
like a map showing her story.
When the pain of her growing up became too much,
she told me of how she disliked it.

I do not like to indulge in the idea of playing with fate.
Everything happens the way it's supposed to; divinely timed.
But I often find myself lost in the a daydreams of us being what we once were.
I'll collect my hopes and wishes and put them aside.
I'll burn them, set them alight;
watch as everything I have ever wanted flamed into nothingness.
But the flames danced in the shapes of my happiness.
The memories silhouetted in the fires,
they burn my eyes open;
to torment me with what could have been.
Who knew I'd see hope in the very thing that destroys this world?

Every birthday wish.
Every 11:11.
Every coin thrown in a fountain.
Every single time.
It was you.

There is nothing poetic about me,
I can romanticise only so much.
But my story isn't one of beauty or elegance.
I could glorify the pain I feel,
but in fact the pain I feel only hurts.
I just need to cry.

– nothing left to write

I wonder how long I must live for me to not connect everything with you.
How long will it be?
Before I stop speaking to the stars about you.
Before I stop taking pictures of the sky because they remind me of you.
Before I go to bed at night hoping to wake up anywhere but here.
How long?

Even if I could turn the clock,
reverse time,
return to the chapters before you,
I don't think I'd change anything.
Because even after all this, I'm not willing to rip out all those pages.
Despite them being filled with forgotten promises and empty hearts,
they're all I have of you.
If the only thing I have is the idea of you, then I'd rather have that than not have you at all.

– co-dependent

I can't guarantee that you'll be in every chapter of my life.
Maybe you're only here for this one,
or perhaps we'll meet again in the following pages.
But if not?
The moonshine from the night we met will be the ink I write my story with.
You'll be with me every step of the way;
even if you're not really.

The devil himself plucked my dreams from my open mind.
What I'd done to deserve this,
I'll never know.
He granted the wishes to those who'd aspire the same as I and giggled to himself as I watched them live my fantasy.
This life is a game,
and the devil is a foul player.

Until the day I am her,
I'll be envious of the me that has you.
She must feel so alive;
so purposeful.
She is me,
but not quite so.
Our hearts don't beat the same,
because when you told her you loved her,
that heart of hers would've stopped for a moment.
A split second rippling through history,
changing the course of her life forever.

So I'll always be envious of the me that is a heartbeat behind.

Detaching from the person you were supposed to stay with forever
really destroys you.
The feeling of unravelling our souls from one another was brutal.
When they were the person who gave you a reason to live another day,
you can't help but feel purposeless without them.
I never thought I'd see the day when all I have of you is memories.
The little corner in my heart you sat in is now just a hollow shell
of something that could've been so much more.

We were a love never finished.
Our hearts never quite fill to the brim for each other.
Our hands never did meet.
Our souls could've had much more.
Like picking a flower before it had bloomed,
we were thieved of our ending.
We were written in the stars from the beginning;
but even the stars die out eventually.

I don't think of you.
Not that often anyways.
I have a life that I am living and the past is very much, in the past.
I am too sweetened with the fruits of life to ever think about you.
But when I am alone,
and there is nothing to think about except thoughts,
you somehow return.
Not in a way that is melancholic.
Just the recollection of you,
and me,
and us.
I just sit, and wonder.

– night wonders

You taste of butterflies in my tummy.
Or the sensation of dancing with not a single care in the world.
You taste of late summer evening walks.
Or early morning sunrises.
You taste of every good there is.
You are treat.
Something I can only indulge in once in a while.
Like a little something to keep me alive.
But the bottle is emptied.
And the last taste of you running down my throat will be the sweetest pain I'll ever get.

I knew that from the moment I looked up at the sky and
didn't think of you, our time was up.
I had lost any sense of home when I saw the universe.
All those stars and planets and cosmos;
I didn't feel a thing.
A part of my soul left when my love for you did.

Oh, God you were perfect.
You were my everything.
You were my sun,
and my moon.
You were the gravity tying me to this very earth.

We weren't going to end in a heartbreak or tragedy.
The saddest grief I am to live isn't the one caused by the end of a love story,
but rather one that never began.

– an empty story

Somewhere out there, we have it all.
Just beyond the horizon,
a little further than the stars,
is a place for us.
I know that the me and you that in that place are okay.
Even if I don't have the satisfaction of a forever with you,
then at least I have the peace in knowing that at least one version of me can know you.

I'll love you, in every universe.
Even if you'll never realise.

I've filled more pages about you,
than you'd ever imagine.
Stacks and stacks of poems about every word I wish I could say.
But I will never know when to shut the book.
When do I finally lay to rest this idea?
I do not have a forever to spare,
to wait for a day I'll finally speak this poetry,
a day I cannot guarantee.
Writing about you has changed my outlook on this life forever.
But it's high time I let your story rest.

– what a wonderful read you were.

Chapter 3

Asiatic Lilies – travels

She is someone I'll never be.
She is so pure, so untouched.
Oh, to be so protected from the world the way she is.
Your arms serve as a soldiery,
valiantly sheltering her little heart from the wars of the world.
Even as she grows, you'll never fail to stretch yourself so far,
that even the suns from other worlds are shadowed it's mightiness.

– The me that you held

You're the unseen soul that homes my whispers.
Every echo of my love is kept within your mind.
It is you and I,
and I and you.
You listen to me as I unravel the endless thoughts knotted in me.
You sit,
you glow,
you admire me.
It is not a romance or a love of any kind.
It is a kindness,
a warmth that no sun could give me.

If it will be so, that I never find your soul,
I know you will watch me on the nights I dream of you.
If the skies are clear, and the rain finally stops,
you will see me.
I will slumber under your light, too lost
in the depth of your absence, to notice your presence.
You never existed in my world, so I found you in another.
The bitter idea of not being enough for you to stay,
empties a part of me,
I didn't know needed to be full.
So, I will wish upon a star every time I see you glowing extra bright,
in hopes that one day I will meet your gaze,
in a world we both know.

– moon

I will not settle for a life without you.
I will not stop trying until I experience you.
Even if it doesn't work out, even if it rips me up.
I am okay with not having forever with you, but to exist in a life
where I will never know you is something I simply cannot abide by.
I will break those rules set by the gods.
Snap every law of physics known to mankind if it means I'll have an attempt at you.

I truly do see you wherever I look.
The clouds form in such synchronicity that they silhouette you.
Those burning rocks that haunt the sky align in ways that shape your name.
Though you do not inhabit this world,
it is almost as though you speak through it.
The wind somehow whispers to me,
your name nipping on my ears.
Or the oranges and yellows of sunflowers and buttercups reminding me of your colours far too often.
I truly do see you wherever I look.

– homesick

We had a forever waiting for us.
The worlds were ours;
ours alone.
But you beat me to it and now wake every day in a different life.
That's all I could've ever hoped for you.
Never staying in one place too long;
you've got so much to see.
I however,
will take refuge in a corner of the world.
I'll be okay with everything I am and everything I cannot be
But while you're writing your name into the stars,
I'll be planting lily flowers.
So that even if I don't get to see you grow,
I've got a part of you with
me.

I have wandered this world alone,
for as long as time can tell.
But even as the sun rises and seasons change,
I find a home in the comets and cosmos.
The night time sky is much more to me than just a pretty view;
because while I walk this lonely earth,
I know that I am built from star dust and constellations.
At least I can look to the sky and see a place for me,
as the child of the stars and the moon.

I like to think,
on the days when the sunrise is extra orange in the mornings
or the nights when the moon is shining extra bright,
that it's them.
Like the universe knows.
It sees me, rooting me on.
Reminders to me that all the good I am deserving of,
is waiting for me somewhere beautiful.

The empty souls of people passed
watch our hearts collide.
Their hollow eyes fill with tears of longing for a love like ours.
They curse our names with jealousy;
their screams echo through the infinite.
The whispers of an eternal love embroidered itself into the fabric of time.
We'll watch from the moon while their earth freezes of a loveless life.

My sky is filled with an infinite maybes. an endless view
of everything that might've happened.
The moon holds my secrets and the stars hold my heart.
They stay, they listen,
and love the parts of me that couldn't be loved.

The person reflected in the mirror is my greatest piece of art.
I built her from sticks and stones,
and what an empire she is now.
No matter how much I write,
there will never really be a story like mine.
It's not romantic, or thrilling.
It's just a tale of a soul not quite meant for here,
finding her place in this world.

Chapter 4

Lavender – Healing

Death will inevitably take me one day.
And maybe I won't have picked every flower,
or seen every sunset, but I am sure I'll be ready.
My soul will go back home to the place I belong.
Even if I spend my entire life in a world I was never supposed to be in,
at least I will exist in entire death with the comfort of a home no one knows.

You were more of a family to me in the short time we had,
than those who built me from their own flesh and bones.
We weren't ever blood, but parts of you flow through my veins;
and always will.

Not everything was meant to be forever.
As much as I' d like to keep you behind glass, or preserved in resin, I can't.
Even if it is for a moment, a brief second, just to witness you.
Alive.
That instant where it is only me observing you for everything you are,
your perfections will be preserved in my mind.
So, I needn't wrap you in cotton.
Or pin and frame you.
Sometimes it is better to behold a flower for its simple beauty,
instead of picking it to carry its short lived magnificence.

I wonder if flowers grow where we once were.
I'd like to think that even if we couldn't grow together and bloom
into the people we were always meant to be, *together*,
then maybe perhaps something else could thrive in our place.

This peaceful goodbye is a chapter in my life I so dreaded.
We have beautifully outgrown each other.
We no longer exist how we did before.
Our leaves aren't the same shades of green anymore.
Our vines are taking different pathways.
We're finally blooming into the artistry we we're always meant to be.
Our roots will always be interwoven,
but you are a sunflower
and I am a rose.

I'll never thank you enough.
For protecting her from the side of life I got to know.
Thank you,
for giving her the life she so rightly deserves.
Thank you,
for having a home of love and happiness.
Thank you,
for giving me a home worth returning to.

You are safe now.
You'll exist somewhere I'll never quite know.
But I hope it's as perfect as you deserve.
I hope there are butterflies for you to chase.
Or a library for you to read endlessly.
I hope there is magic there.
Perhaps,
in the literal sense,
in a way that you can wave a wand and everything is yours.
Or in the way that you see the beauty whatever world you live in now.

Do not make me a lover of the stars.
Or someone who must have conversations with the moon
just to talk to you.
Do not give a reason to linger a little longer after the sun sets.
Do not give me a reason to have the ache of missing my person.
I will listen to your struggles on a loop for the entirety of my life
if it means I get to keep you here.

You healed a heart you did not break.
You listened to its cries and whispered back sweet nothingness.
You held it in your hands like you were holding the world.
You brought back to life something I believed to be long ago dead.
I thank those who broke it in the first place,
because I will not have had the honour of being loved by you.

The place you have in this world is one that only you can fill.
The world does not spin this fast,
the sun does not burn this wildly,
the stars do not glow so bright,
for you to feel as though you are not enough.
They do their utter most to make this life that more bearable for you.
Because you the sweetest soul who deserves only the very best this,
and every other, world has to offer.

The human race is remarkable.
We've travelled to the stars,
we have done the impossible.
But to explain with words the sensation of falling
for someone in a way that the human brain can mentally fathom
is still to be done.
There is yet to be a combination of letters that utterly envelops
the feeling of finding your person.
While I do have other accomplishments I intend to fulfil,
my way with words is my gift and so my intentions for this life
is to find those perfect lyrics that'll leave my mark on the world.

I'll continue to stare at the reflection in the mirror until
I have become the very person I promised to you I'd be.
someone far greater than you.
Although I was assembled from the parts of you, you no longer needed,
I'll be worth far more than you ever will.
I am built from your scraps and ruins,
but I am artistry that people admire.

Thank you for somehow keeping me here.
Thank you,
for letting me live through the nights that I wanted to be my last.
Thank you,
For giving me a purpose, even when I felt purposeless.
Thank you,
for the existence I get to have.
And a final thank you, for you finally sending me home.
I am truly lucky to have been given this life,
even if it is but one of many I am to live.

"You've become such a beautiful person.
I am, so proud of you".

On the days I cannot, may the sun be your warmth,
your bedsheets be what hold you on the nights you can't sleep.
May the wind whisper sweet nothings in your ear,
and knowing the fact that I'll be home soon,
be that little bit of motivation to live another day.

There is nothing greater the feeling than the feeling of acceptance.
The feeling of looking the mirror and being happy with how you look.
The feeling of finally taking care of yourself, not to change the way you look, but to grow.
I could not be more proud of myself for finally being that person.

What makes you that little bit more extraordinary than the rest of them,
is the fact you're still going.
You're still fighting despite everything.
You know deep down that you're destined for far greater things.
Yes, you were brought to this life for a reason,
but that doesn't mean you have to settle for it.
And if you choose to, that's okay.
But if not?
I wish you the best of luck on your journey.

Although we are so opposing,
the roots our souls have,
are entirely the same.
You and I both ran from the battles we knew we couldn't win.
We hid amongst the shadows of a thousand maybes,
and lost ourselves in the adventures of running.
Our unfinished wars haunt us,
we know we cannot run forever.
But what differs between you and I,
is that although it will destroy everything that I am,
I will face this.

The person I am meant to be is someone I am not; so, I must grow.

I think I'm going to be okay.
It feels weird for me to admit it.
Because I honestly thought I'd never say those words and mean it.
But, I'm prepared for what lies ahead,
the ups,
the downs,
the days where nothing happens at all.
And I am okay with that.
I'm prepared for the fact that this life has such amazing things stored for me.

I really do think I'll be okay.

You can rest now.
I'll lay you down on a bed daisies and paint your fingernails purple.
Don't worry, puddles is with you too.
I'll Whisper to you, the lullaby's that'll calm your mind; we both know which ones those are.
I'll stroke your hair until every last star in the beautiful head of yours burns out.
I'll forever be in debt to those little lights.
They kept us around for a lot longer than we both anticipated.
You have fought this life valiantly; you deserve nothing but peace.
But it is your time,
your sun is setting and your stars are finally blooming.
So goodnight, my angel,
you were greatest warrior princess the world ever saw.

– littlest me

About the Author

Hi, I'm Charlie! I've been an enthusiastic writer for as long as I can remember, hence the book.

As you can tell from the poems and what they're about, I've had a variety of experiences, and writing was what got me through a lot of those times!

This book is an insight to the journey I've been through and the beauty I choose to create from that.

I hope you enjoy this as much as I did.

Authors Note

This book is for the people who can't explain how they feel, the ones who were never listened to and those who are still sat in silence.

This book is for the ones who hurt.

I wrote these poems at a time when my hurt demanded to be felt. Instead of the expected things teens do to cope with the stress of their lives, I wrote. Oddly enough, I found out I was actually quite good at it. So, this is when my book began.

There is all kinds of hurts and healings in here. I hope you find some sense of familiarity and hope when you read my work.

And that, even when the days seem endless, you *can* survive.

www.ingramcontent.com/pod-product-compliance
Ingram Content Group UK Ltd.
Pitfield, Milton Keynes, MK11 3LW, UK
UKHW032318150125
453757UK00001B/7

9 781803 819167